The Old Road to Paradise by Margaret Widdemer

I0162985

TO MOTHER, WITH MARGARET'S LOVE

Margaret Widdemer was born on September 30th, 1884 in Doylestown, Pennsylvania, and grew up in Asbury Park, New Jersey.

She graduated from the Drexel Institute Library School in 1909.

Margaret first gained recognition with her poem 'The Factories', and its subject of child labor.

In 1919, she married Robert Haven Schauffler, a widower five years her senior who was an author and cellist and published widely on poetry, travel, culture, and music.

That same year she won the Pulitzer Prize (then still known as the Columbia University Prize) for this collection 'The Old Road to Paradise'. The award was shared with Carl Sandburg for 'Cornhuskers'.

Margaret's career was long and prolific covering poetry, adult and children's fiction and some self-help guidance books. Her friendships covered such authors as Ezra Pound, F. Scott Fitzgerald, T. S. Eliot, Thornton Wilder, and Edna St. Vincent Millay.

Margaret Widdemer died in New York City, on July 14th, 1978.

Index of Contents

THE OLD ROAD TO PARADISE

Ours is a dark Easter-tide,
  And a scarlet Spring,
But high up at Heaven-Gate
  All the saints sing,
Glad for the great companies
  Returning to their King.

Oh, in youth the dawn's a rose,
  Dusk's an amethyst,
All the roads from dusk to dawn
  Gay they wind and twist;
The old road to Paradise
  Easy it is missed!

But out on the wet battlefields,
  Few the roadways wind,
One to grief, one to death
  No road that's kind–
The old road to Paradise

Plain it is to find!

(Martin in his Colonel's cloak,
  Joan in her mail,
David with his crown and sword—
  None there be that fail—
Down the road to Paradise
  Stand to greet and hail!)

Where the dark's a terror-thing,
  Morn a hope doubt-tossed.
Where the lads lie thinking long
  Out in rain and frost,
There they find their God again,
  Long ago they lost:

Where the night comes cruelly,
  Where the hurt men moan,
Where the crushed forgotten ones
  Whisper prayers alone,
Christ along the battlefields
  Comes to lead His own:

Souls that would have withered soon
  In the hot world's glare,
Blown and gone like shriveled things,
  Dusty on the air,
Rank on rank they follow Him,
  Young and strong and fair!

Ours is a sad Easter-tide,
  And a woeful day,
But high up at Heaven-Gate
  The saints are all gay,
For the old road to Paradise,
  That's a crowded way!

THE OLD KINGS

All of the Old Kings
  Are wakened from their sleep,
Arthur out of Avalon,
  Ogier from the deep,
Redbeard from his Dragon-Rock,
  Sigurd from his fen . . .
"Is it time," they rise and cry,
  "To lead our hosts again?"

They have donned their wingéd helms,
  They would rise and reign,
The young king Sebastian,
  The old king Charlemagne,
Harold with his great bow,
  Roland with his horn . . .
Men have heard their horses' hoofs
  Many a scarlet morn!

The Old Kings have risen . . .
  Where the hosts advance
Redbeard cries his Germans on,
  Karle cries out for France,
Up and down the battlefield
  Ghostly armies beat,
Stilly down the gray sea glides
  Olaf's shadow-fleet:

Up and down the red fields
  Men have seen them go,
Seen the long plumes on the wind,
  Seen the pennons flow,

Harry out of Agincourt
  Sends his bowmen wide,
Joan that has forgiven them
  Battles at their side. . . .

Christ, king of Paradise,
  Hasten with Thy hosts,
Angels all in silver mail,
  Saints and blessed ghosts,
Cry the long swords sheathed again,
  Cry the pennons furled,
Lest under Ragnarok
  Lie the shattered world!

ST. JEANNE RIDES OUT

(For Amy Lowell)

St. Jeanne she sat with Michaël,
With Marguerite and Raphaël,
And all the saints who sent her forth a many years ago,
And high behind her gold-ringed head,
The martyrs dressed in white and red
And seraphim all silver-winged they chanted row on row.

St. Jeanne she spoke to Michaël,
To Marguerite and Raphaël,
"Oh, here's no place for such as I, all white and gold and warm,
For I was but a peasant maid
Strong of arm and unafraid,
Before you sent me garnering along the battle-storm."

St. Jeanne she's laid her garlands by,
Her crown and palm that glittered high

And all the golden trinketry she won at Heaven Gate,
She's out along by Mary's Street
Where little stars lie thick and sweet,
With helm and sword they took from her at Rouen-Town of late.

St. Peter swore, "The gate stands wide,
So many folk have marched inside—
I'll drop my golden keys tonight and snatch a sword again!"
And stalwart saints and martyrs all
And sworded angels silver-tall
In straight and shining companies they've followed in her train.

And down the fields of Paradise
The churchmen all so great and wise
Who won to Heaven so hardly once, they've knelt to her at last,
All they who laughed at Rouen-Town
To see the flames beat up and down
And learned her for a saint that day, they follow glad and fast.

Oh, did you hear the shouting then?
Along the fields of weary men
There's lifted heart and strengthened arm and laughing glad accord:
Oh, who may doubt what end may be?
With all her wingéd chivalry
St. Jeanne rides down her fields tonight to battle for the Lord!

A BALLAD OF THE WISE MEN

The Christ-Child lay in Bethlehem
  And the Wise Men gave Him gold,
And Mary-Mother she hearkened them
  As they prayed in the cattle-fold:
"Smile then, smile, little Prince of Earth,
  Smile in Thy holy sleep,

Now Thou art come, for want and dearth
There shall be plenty and light and mirth
  Through lands where the poor folk weep."
But Mary-Mother was still and pale
  And she raised her golden-ringed head,
"Then why have I heard the children wail
All night long on the far-blown gale
While my own Child slept?" she said.
(But far overhead the angels sang:
"There shall be joy!" the clear notes rang!)

The Christ-Child lay in Bethlehem
  And the censers burned for him
That the Wise Men swung on its silver stem
  And prayed while the smoke rose dim:
"Sleep, then sleep, little Son of God,
  Sleep while the whole world prays;
All the world shall fear Thy nod,
Following close Thy staff and rod,
  Praising this day of days."
But Mary-Mother turned whispering
  There by the manger-bed
"Then why do I hear the mocking ring
Of voices crying and questioning
  Through the scented smoke?" she said.
(But high overhead the angels sang—
"There shall be faith!" the pure notes rang.)
The Christ-Child lay in Bethlehem
  And the Wise Men gave Him myrrh,
And Mary-Mother she hearkened them
  As they prayed by the heart of her:
"Sleep, then sleep, little Prince of Peace,
  Sleep, take Thy holy rest,
Now Thou art come all wars shall cease,
Thou who hast brought all strife release
  Even from east to west!"

But Mary-Mother she veiled her head
  As if her great joys were lost,
And "Here is only a manger-bed,
Then why do I hear clashed swords?" she said.
"And why do I see the tide of red
  Over the whole world tossed?"
(But still overhead the angels sang:
"There shall be peace!" the sure notes rang!)

NEXT YEAR

Up and down the street I know,
  Now that there are Grief and War,
All day long the people go
  As they went before;

But when now the lads go by—
  Careless look and careless glance—
My heart wonders—"Which shall lie
  Still next year in France?"

When the girls go fluttering—
  Flushing cheek and tossing head—
My heart asks—"Next year shall bring
  Which a lover dead?"

Lord, let peace be kind and fleet—
  Put an end to Grief and War;
Let them walk the little street
  Careless as before!

HOMES

The lamplight's shaded rose
On couch and chair and wall,
The drowsy book let fall,
The children's heads, bent close
In some deep argument,
The kitten, sleepy-curled,
Sure of our good intent,
The hearth-fire's crackling glow:
His step that crisps the snow,
His laughing kiss, wind-cold. . . .

Only the very old
Gifts that the night-star brings,
Dear homely evening-things,
Dear things of all the world,
And yet my throat locks tight . . .

Somewhere far off I know
Are ashes on red snow
That were a home last night.

FATHER PRAYER

Lord God, Who let Your baby son
  Pass earthward where the joys were few
To a hard death when all was done,
  And very far away from You;

My little lad must go today
  Paths where I cannot guide his feet,
Through dangers that I cannot stay
  To strife I cannot help him meet;

He has heard voices calling him
  Though youth is gay and life is warm,
And right seems far away and dim,
  To weary ways and battle-storm:

Lord God, Whose Son went steadily
  Down the hard road He had to tread,
Guard my son too, that he may be
  Strong in his hours of doubt and dread!

GOOD-BY, MY LOVER

All the flags stream abroad, and the crowds wave and cry–
And I watch for your face in the long lines marching by;

For my lips bade you go, but my heart would bid you stay–
Oh, lad, and will the war be long, and you so far away?

And your step as you marched, would it lag or fall more true
If you know that my heart's gone to war to follow you?

POEM FOR A PICTURE

(Children at play on a French Battlefield)

"When I was a child,"
  You shall tell one day,
Children, on these blackened fields
  Gallantly at play,
"All the quiet sky
  Burst in death aflame;
One day, I was young,

Then . . . The Horror came."

"When I was a child . . ."
  Wind-tossed leaves of war,
Is there childhood still for you,
  Wise in horror-lore,
Who have heard your sisters' screams
  Shattering your play,
Seen your mothers past their dead
  Led to shame away?

Ragged, helpless, maimed,
  Hungry, left alone
Where the smoking roof-beams lie
  By the wrecked hearth-stone,
Still you mime (child-hearts are strong,
  Childhood pain is brief)
Echoes of world-victory,
  World-defeat, world-grief!
Dauntless in your rags,
  Insolent in mirth,
Laughing with young lips that know
  All the griefs of earth,
God, who loves a high heart well,
  Will not let you fail–
You are France, who laughs at Hell–
  France, who shall prevail!

PRAYER FOR THE NEW YEAR

Lord God, we lift to Thee
  A world hurt sore.
Look down, and let it be
  Wounded no more!

Lord, when this year is done
  That wakes today
Many shall pray to Thee
  Who do not pray;

Let all lips comfort them,
  All hearts be kind,
They who this year shall leave
  Their joys behind:

Give them Thy comforting,
  Help them to know
That though their hopes are gone
  Thou dost not go;

They who shall give for Thee
  Lover and son,
Show them Thy world set free,
  Thy battles done!

Lord God, we lift to Thee
  A world in pain,
Look down and let it be
  Made whole again!

THE SINGING WOOD

THE GRAY MAGICIAN

I was living very merrily on Middle Earth
  As merry as a maid may be
Till the Gray Magician came down along the road
  And flung his cobweb cloak on me:

14

His cobweb cloak of gray brushed my eyes and my ears
  And all the curtained air was thinned,
And I came to the sight of the quiet Other People
  Who live in the water and the wind:
And I cannot go abroad to gather up the faggots,
  Singing to the honest air
Because of the fingers of the brown wood-women
  Catching at my blowing hair:

And I cannot sit at home and be quiet at my spinning,
  Singing to the thread I spin,
Because of the crying of the green sea-women
  Beneath my sill to be let in:

And I wish the Gray Magician had been swung to an oak
  Or drowned in the deep green sea
Before he brushed my face with his cobweb cloak
  And stole the Middle Earth from me!

THE DANCERS

(For Edwin Arlington Robinson)

Ours was a quiet town, a still town, a sober town,
Softly curled the yellow roads that slept in the sun,
Staid came the day up and staid came the night down
And staidly went we sleepwise when the day's work was done!

Oh, they came dancing down, the gay ones, the bonny ones,
We had never seen the like, sweet and wild and glad,
Down the long roads they came, fluting and dancing,
Flowers in each lass's hair and plumes on each lad!

Sweet were their clinging hands, kind were their voices,

"Dance with us, laugh with us, good grave folk," said they,
"Swift we must go from you, time's long for toiling,
Come and make joy with us the brief while we stay!"

Oh, then was a gay time, a wild time, a glad time,
Hand in hand we danced with them beneath sun and moon,
Flowers were for garlanding and greens were for dancing—
This was the wisdom we learned of them too soon!

Swift went the day past, a glad day, a wild day,
Swift went the night past, a night wild and glad,
Down fell their arms from us, loosening, fleeting,
Far down the roads they danced, wild lass and wild lad!

Far fled their dancing feet, far rang their laughter,
Far gleamed their mocking eyes beneath the garlands gay,
All too late we knew them then, the wild eyes, the elf-eyes,
Wood-folk and faun-folk that danced our hearts away!

Ours is a still town, a sad town, a sober town,
Still lie the dun roads all empty in the sun,
Sad comes the day up and sad falls the night down,
And sadly go we sleepwise when the day's watch is done!

THE GYPSY STAR

There were seven shining stars that swung above my cradle
  (She never was kind to me, Diana our Lady the Moon!)
And one was rosy-pale, and one was scarlet-golden,
  And one was a little shadowed star that only could vanish soon!

Oh, Mars was scarlet-wild and Venus was veiled in shadow
  (She called to the clouds to come, Diana our Lady of Snow!)
But all of the stars that rose and helped me where I must wander

They never could hold the Gypsy Star to the roads where my feet
must go!

Oh, one was a star of crowns and one was a star of dreaming
  And one was a star of mockery and one was a help from pain,
And ever the Sun was kind and shone for my idle singing,
  But ah, my wandering Gypsy Star I never shall find again!

Oh, Mars may burn to dusk and Venus may rise from shadow
  And even the Moon that hated me forget as she lifts the tide,
Yet what if they gleam or fade, and what if they stay or wander? . . .
  Alas, my wandering Gypsy Star that faded and flamed and died!

THE FAUN'S SWEETHEART

We met by the Wood of Doom,
Day gone and the dusk come after . . .
And I thought you were one like the lads anear,
Only more glad and fair,
Till I heard you laugh in the gloom
And I knew a faun's wild laughter–
But oh, it was all too late to fear
The little horns in your hair!

Far back leaped the woodlights' glow,
And you fled–and I might not follow,
And I loosed the hold of your hurrying hand
At the piercing wood-flutes' call;
For my human feet fell slow,
Flagging at hill and hollow,
Till far rang back from the leaping band
The click of your light footfall.

The days pass long and still

Where I sit still at my spinning . . .
But I wish the sounds of the talking stream
Would hush, and I might not know
Over the forest-hill
The sounds of the night's beginning,
Nor see the flit of the hurrying gleam
Where the lightfoot woodfolk go!

For I cannot have hope in heaven
To quiet my heartache after,
Because you were only a faun o' the wood
With never a soul at all.
And never the hills of heaven
May echo a faun's wild laughter
Nor over the harpstrings' holy flood
Sound ringing your light footfall!

DREAM-HOUSE

(For Anna Hempstead Branch)

I went to the house of the Lady of Dreams
  For a dream to carry away
That should ferry me over the blackest streams
  I had to cross by day;

For comforting dreams from her small white hands
  Rise up like butterflies,
And dreams like the lakes in old fairylands
  Lie back of her shining eyes,

And gold-riddled dreams like tapestries
  Cling painted along her walls
And yellow bird-dreams from shadow-trees

Come fluttering when she calls;

And all of the day-dark when she spoke
  Was shattered and rainbow-hung,
And she gave me a dream like a scarlet cloak
  And a dream like a wreath rose-strung . . .

But I went from the house of the Lady of Dreams
  And my packet of dreams blew wide,
And only a red-rose cloud in streams
  Swung torn in the west outside!

GARDEN DREAM

They cried before my gate at morning-mirth,
"Come out and help us burn the weeds from earth!"

But I was planting out my garden-close
With wands of lily and with slips of rose,
And their scented wavings made the air so sweet
That I could not listen to the trampling feet . . .
(Yet there blew a perfume from the garden-bed
That changed the evil weeds to white and red!)

They called before my gate at noontide-breath,
"Come out and help us check the dance of death!"

But I was dancing in a woodland ring
With brown wood-women for my partnering,
And fauns that fluted till the green glades rang,
And all I heard was what the wood-birds sang. . . .
(Yet there came a music from the wood-folk's flute
That made the drums of evil kind and mute!)

They cried before my gate at sweet of night,
"Come out and help us scourge the black world white!"

But I was weaving me a golden gown
All strung with silver lilies up and down

With moon-white laces that should foam and fall,
And I could not hear their lashing words at all . . .
(Yet there streamed a light from out the golden gown
That cleansed the blackness of each evil town!)
And every poor man had a garden-close
With wands of lilies and with slips of rose,
And every poor child danced the woodlands through
And sang and fluted merry songs he knew,
And every woman had a golden gown
Gay-strung with silver ribbons up and down,
And we all went singing how the world is fair
And warm the summer light and sweet the air!

SWAN-CHILD

(For Aline)

My feet have touched the Dancing Water,
  My lips have kissed the Singing Rose
And I was born a swan-girl's daughter . . .
Oh, I would stay with you, my lover,
  But in my heart a sea wind blows
And in the dark the wild swans hover . . .
Tonight as I went down to sea
  To cast my net, to draw my net,
The Marsh-King's daughter whispered me,
  "Sister," she called, "do you forget?"
For though I am a fisher's child

It was a swan-maid mothered me,
And I have wings that I can don
When day is done, when dark comes on,
  To bear me high across the sea.

One star-dusk when I waited you
  And it was long before you came,
There was a bird with wings of blue
  And claws of gold and crest of flame
Who sang with words as mortals do:
  He sang me of an ivory fountain
  Within a wood beyond a mountain

Where lies beneath the water's flow
  A golden key, a silver cup,
  Until my hand shall lift them up . . .
  (Oh, I must go from you, my lover!)
For they were mine once long ago.
How shall you keep me, dear my lover?
  My heart is yours till night-winds call,
And then dear earth-things fade and fall
  (Oh, I was born a swan-girl's daughter!)
For I have found beneath the moon
Brown fairy fernseed for my shoon
  That carries me where no man knows,
Beyond the sands, beyond the clover . . .
I cannot bide with you, my lover . . .
  My feet have touched the Dancing Water,
  My lips have kissed the Singing Rose.

CHANGELING

Though she has a name you bore,
Elfin-Heart we loved before,

21

You are lost to us, you child,
Little life-flame burning wild!
Though her hair–how like!– is tossed
Like your yellow head that's lost,
And her blue eyes seem to smile
Like yours lost this weary while,
This dim woman lifelessly
Playing you–you are not she!
You that were a wisp, a spark,
Small wild sunray, Gleam-in-Dark,
Never you, wild heart awing,
This that is a changeling!

Elfin-Heart, too like you were–
Mocking eyes and tossing hair–
Cruel laughter, changeful ways–
To your kin the wandering fays,
To have passed their hidden ring,
Safe, uncaught, unfollowing!
Somewhere in a green hill's heart
Elfin-tall you laugh apart
Where forever cold and gay
Do the Strange Folk's pipers play . . .

And while this that bears your seeming
Goes among us dumb and dreaming
You dance on eternally
With the Dark Queen's chivalry!

SONGS FROM A MASQUE

THE WOODFOLK SWEEP THROUGH

The Water-Spirit:

22

Water flows in the wild wood deep,
  Dreamy water that slips and sighs,
I shall whisper your heart to sleep,
  Flowing down on your lips and eyes—
Dance and dream–dance and dream—
Folk of woodland and tree and stream!

The Fire-Spirit
Fire shall burn and be always new,
  Flames leap wild on the flashing air;
I shall sweep from the heart of you,
  Worldly fever of love and care—
Dance and leap– dance and leap—
Folk of woodland and wind and steep!

The Earth-Spirit
Earth is kind in the peace of night,
  Earth that loves when all else is done—
I will hide you at loss of light
  Deep from the hurt of the snow or sun—
Dance till night– dance till night—
Folk of woodland and vale and height!

Chorus of Woodfolk
Wild the heart of the magic wood,
  Wild the dream that shall never stay,
Flute and laughter and dance are good,
  Joy and singing the while we may—
Joy is good–joy is good—
Folk of river and field and wood!

Swanhild Sings Unseen
White wings, far wings,
  Fade down the sky,
Dream things, fair things
  Follow and fly;

Young heart, wild heart,
  Ah, could you follow
All the clouds, all the dreams,
  Down the world's hollow!

Swanhild Sings to the Knight
What shall I do with my heart,
  That will not go with thee,
Lover of mine, knight of mine,
  Guide to the heights afar?

There is a dream to follow
  That will not let me be—
I must go down to the marshland's water,
  Hiding from wind and star!
What shall I do with thy heart,
  Seeking me without rest,
I who must strip all hands from me,
  Guarding my steps in fear!
Turn from the fairy woodland,
  Pass to thy holy quest—
I must go seek for the track of the swan
  And the sound of the step of the deer!

UNSPELLED

The world of dream is shattered; hill and tree
  And wingéd music and enchanted lawn;
For someone signed the cross, and suddenly
  Our faëryland was gone:

The dark fell swiftly on the fear-struck land
  And mocking echoes cried across the chill;

The wailing woodfolk fled us . . . but your hand
  Held close to my hand still.

Oh, what are woodland dream and fluting reed,
  Red glamor of enchanted jewel-stone?
I pass the ruined faëry-gates indeed . . .
  But not alone.

THE SINGING WOOD

I followed far from the roadway
  After my golden ball
(How could I tell the way it went
  Where it might lie or fall?)
And coaxing vines from the Singing Wood
  Came twining around my feet
And scent of flowers from the Singing Wood
  Oh, it was sweet, was sweet!

Once I met a satyr,
  Once I was with a faun,
Once I spoke with a woman o' doom
  Spinning from dusk till dawn,
Once I followed a will-o'-the-wisp
  Dancing along the fen . . .
Never the sun in the Singing Wood
  Never a bird-loud glen!

All the trees were sighing,
  All of the brooks were tears,
All of the flowers were bleeding-hearts
  Scarlet with hopes and fears,
All of the vines were hands that clung
  Twisting about my heart . . .

Oh, the thorns of the Singing Wood
  Sharp they can tear and smart!

I might have won to the rainbow's end,
  But never for all o' me
Shall my feet stray into the Singing Wood
  For any fair things that flee . . .
Here on earth are the day and night,
  Human women and men–
And oh, 'tis good to be out o' the wood,
  Into the world again!

BEING YOUNG

WHISTLE-FANTASY

Out in the dark the train passes
And the whistle calls to the child,
Desolate, piercing, wild,
From the track in the meadow-grasses . . .
"Far, far away," it screams,
"Far, far away,
Out in the distance are dreams
Dreams you shall follow some day
Far through the endless wild . . .
Distance . . . dreams . . ."
Backward the faint call streams:
Far in the dark the train passes,
And the whistle calls to the child.

ONCE WHEN WE BOUGHT VALENTINES

(For Kenneth)

Close upon the window-glass pressed our eager faces—
Hearts and torches all aflare, frame on frame of laces,
Wreathing roses all abloom, Cupids all awing,
Valentines—and valentines! swung along the string,
Lights from out the window-pane glinted on the snow
Once when we bought valentines—how long, how long ago!

Slow we tiptoed in the shop, scarlet-cheeked and shy,
Half-elate, half-afraid to be asked to buy,
Sidling toward the prettiest on their swaying strings,
Laughing at the ugliest, monstrous painted things.
(Still the little thrill of fear—life was strange, you knew—
What if someone sometime sent one of those to you?)

Tense we watched the lagging mail, furtive hearts abeat . . .
Surely it would never come down the endless street!
Surely all the valentines would be gone before
(Out of sight, into sight) it could reach our door.

Surely all the envelopes sealed with hearts of red
(Were they there? Were they ours?) would be gone instead!
Hearts and doves, wreaths and loves wonderful to see!
Could He mean the shiny words, "I Can Love But Thee?"
Would he look across the desks when next morning came,
He who sent (If He sent) all those hearts aflame?
Would He know the straggling hand, all in print and bent
Up and down on the folds of the one you sent?

We're too old to buy them now—all the loves and laces,
We can only watch above other little faces.
Glowing at the prettiest, laughing at the plain,
Still the eager faces crowd by the lighted pane.
Once we too saw wonderlights glinting on the snow,
Once we too bought valentines—too long, too long ago!

WHEN I WAS A YOUNG GIRL

(A Song of Old Ballads)

When I was a young girl, all in a green arbor,
  When I was a young girl in Springtimes gone by
All the long days I went singing and smiling,
Down by the roses the sweet days beguiling,
  Love in the arbor and love in the sky . . .
When I was a young girl, a young girl, a young girl,
  When I was a young girl, how happy was I!

Oh, the long days I must sit at my sampler,
  Oh, the slow way that the still time would go!
I longed to be running across the bright heather,
"Off with the silk gown and on with the leather,
  Following the raggle-taggle gypsies, oh!"
When I was a young girl, a young girl, a young girl,
  When I was a young girl, a long time ago!

When I was a young girl in days that were golden,
  When I was a young girl, and life had no smart,
All the world seemed a place for my playing,
Full of great lovers to come to me, saying,
  "Madam, I give you the keys of my heart . . ."
When I was a young girl, a young girl, a young girl,
  When I was a young girl, and dreaming apart!

When I was a young girl, I dreamed of my lover,
  A tall cavalier who should whisper me low,
"Love, on your lips are red roses a-blowing,
I am your true love, and fast is time going
  Am I your true love? Oh, say yes or no!"

When I was a young girl, a young girl, a young girl—
  When I was a young girl, a long time ago!

When I was a young girl there came my true lover,
  Swiftly I knew him in glad days gone by;
Never a sword or a lovelock or feather,
But oh, at his touch 'twas our hearts came together,
  Love in the arbor and love in the sky . . .
When I was a young girl, a young girl, a young girl,
  When I was a young girl, how happy was I!

THE GARDEN

There were many flowers in my mother's garden,
  Sword-leaved gladiolus, taller far than I,
Sticky-leaved petunias, pink and purple-flaring,
  Velvet-painted pansies staring at the sky;

Scentless portulacas crowded down the borders,
  White and scarlet-petaled, satin-rose and gold,
Clustered sweet alyssum, lacy-white and scented,
  Sprays of gray-green lavender to keep till you were old;

In my mother's garden were green-leaved hiding-places,
  Nooks between the lilacs—oh, a pleasant place to play!
Still my heart can hide there, still my eyes can dream it,
  Though the long years lie between and I am far away;

When the world is hard now, when the city's clanging
  Tires my ears and tires my heart and dust lies everywhere,
I can dream the peace still of the soft wind's shining,
  I can be a child still and hide my heart from care.

Lord, if still that garden blossoms in the sunlight,

Grant that children laugh there now among its green and gold,
Grant that little hearts still hide its memoried sweetness,
  Locking one bright dream away for light when they are old!

OCTOBER

Done with the Spring's unrest and gleam,
  The summer's toil and rich unrest,
    With nothing left to seek or keep
    Before she turns to Winter sleep
Earth lays her golden head, to dream
  One month against the gold sky's breast.

HEART OF YOUTH

When I come back in the gloom
To my lighted house once more
My heart says, "Haste tonight!
There is something you do not know,
Something to give you joy,
On the other side of the door
There in the firelight's glow,
There in the lighted room."

My quick heart whispers me,
"The kinsman gone oversea,
The one they have always said
Would surely come back some day,
Waits for you, brown, windblown . . .
Or the lover you have not known
Is waiting you there tonight—
Do you wonder that I rejoice?

Or the dearest one of the dead
Waits in the ring of light
With the old glad face and voice
As if he were never away . . .
Hasten!" my heart has said.

But when I open the door
There are only the old lights
And the old accustomed faces
And the firelight on the floor. . . .

SONG: I WISH I WERE OLD NOW

I wish I were old now,
  And maybe content;
I'd look back the long way
  My footsteps were bent,
And say, "'Tis all done now—
  What odds how it went?"

For all would look smooth then
  And most would look gay,
And "Oh, I was sure then,
  And strong then," I'd say,
And show the wild young things
  My wise-traveled way.

I'd have naught to strive for
  And no thought to form
But how to rest easy
  And how to sleep warm,
And "Pity the poor souls
  Abroad in the storm!"

I wish I were old now
  With living put by,
And peace on the hearthstone
  And peace in the sky,
But–"Oh, to be young now,
  But young now!" they cry!

TO YOUTH AFTER PAIN

What if this year has given
  Grief that some year must bring,
What if it hurt your joyous youth,
  Crippled your laughter's wing?
You always knew it was coming,
  Coming to all, to you,
They always said there was suffering–
  Now it is done, come through.

Even if you have blundered,
  Even if you have sinned,
Still is the steadfast arch of the sky
  And the healing veil of the wind . . .
And after only a little,
  A little of hurt and pain,
You shall have the web of your own old dreams
  Wrapping your heart again.

Only your heart can pity
  Now, where it laughed and passed,
Now you can bend to comfort men,
  One with them all at last,
You shall have back your laughter,
  You shall have back your song,
Only the world is your brother now,

Only your soul is strong!

OLD BOOKS

The people up and down the world that talk and laugh and cry,
They're pleasant when you're young and gay, and life is all to try,
But when your heart is tired and dumb, your soul has need of ease,
There's none like the quiet folk who wait in libraries—
The counselors who never change, the friends who never go,
The old books, the dear books that understand and know!

"Why, this thing was over, child, and that deed was done,"
They say, "When Cleopatra died, two thousand years agone,
And this tale was spun for men and that jest was told
When Sappho was a singing-lass and Greece was very old,
And this thought you hide so close was sung along the wind
The day that young Orlando came a-courting Rosalind!"

The foolish thing that hurt you so your lips could never tell,
Your sister out of Babylon she knows its secret well,
The merriment you could not share with any on the earth
Your brother from King Francis' court he leans to share your mirth,
For all the ways your feet must fare, the roads your heart must go,
The old books, the dear books, they understand and know!

You read your lover's hid heart plain beneath some dead lad's lace,
And in a glass from some Greek tomb you see your own wet face,
For they have stripped from out their souls the thing they could not speak
And strung it to a written song that you might come to seek,
And they have lifted out their hearts when they were beating new
And pinned them on a printed page and given them to you.

The people close behind you, all their hearts are dumb and young,

33

The kindest word they try to say it stumbles on the tongue,
Their hearts are only questing hearts, and though they strive and
try,
Their softest touch may hurt you sore, their best word make you
cry.
But still through all the years that come and all the dreams that go
The old books, the dear books, they understand and know!

THE WIRES

The wires gleamed far and silver,
  Lines on a morning sky;
I heard the white wires singing
  Their song as I went by;
Far and far away they led, and I was bound and young,
And sharp the wind blew overhead, and gave the wires a tongue—
Young folk must wander far,
  Young feet must roam
'Tis a long way to everywhere,
  But oh, a short way home!

The wires gleamed far and golden—
  I followed in their track,
Far and far the gold wires led,
  And never road led back;
Far and far the gold wires went, and oh, I followed fast,
Roads to work ere youth was spent, and joy while youth should last:
Rough roads to fame and gold
  Gay roads to roam,
Roads to hate and roads to love,
  But never roads toward home!

The wires show far and darkened,
  Lines on a sunset sky,

And still the black wires sing me
  Their song as I plod by—
Far and far the black wires wind, and I am old and tired,
And naught is left to seek or find of all that I desired:
Old folk are wise too late,
  Old feet cannot roam,
'Tis a short way to everywhere,
  But oh, a lost way home!

WOMENFOLK

WOMEN

You fret and grieve and turn about
To make this world and living out,
With "This is so" and "That is so—"
Ah, sirs, we learned it long ago!

If you should make an angel tell
What Mary learned of Gabriel
Yet could you know the flaming words
That pierced her with the seven swords?
And if some fiend-snake hissed you low
All he told Eve where God's trees grow,
Yet could you learn the thing she learned
Who sobbing out of Eden turned?

We watched with smiling mother-eyes
The while you stormed, and thought you wise,
At God's great walls, as if you beat
Like babes, with angry hands and feet;
For God, who bound our feet and hands
And laid us under your commands,
Still left us silence, love, and pain,

And dreams to hide and peace to gain. . . .

Why, when you search beyond a doubt
The furthest star's last secret out,

Some woman from her nook shall smile,
Laying her needle down the while,
"Dear, that old dream I told to you?
You smiled . . . I thought you always knew!"
The thing we tell is no new thing,
A wisdom born of suffering,
That there is pain, and there is love,
And God's great silence still above,
And this is all—though you have hurled
Your strength forever on the world.
Quick, let us speak to you, ere yet
Passed from our silence we forget,
Like you, with crowds made deaf and blind,
With dealing close to humankind:
Be swift, for soon we too shall be
With no more place for memory,
Going unfettered as man goes
And scarcely wounded more—who knows?
And all our Vala-dreams shall lift
Like Tyre-smoke and Atlantis-drift . . .

Listen, most dear, the while that we
At once have speech and memory.

EMBROIDERY

She sits and makes pink roses with her thread
And wonders what to do, her heart astir,
What road to take, where roads branch close ahead,

And how to know her true love calling her;
Whether to follow thorny paths (but sweet
The young wild heart's way!) or to fling the door
Wide to love's placid tread with wonted feet,
And how to build her life forevermore.

The rose-sprung needle keeps its darting deft . . .
When life has gone whichever way it goes,
Of all her wonderings shall be only left
The texture and the pattern of this rose:
And when her old eyes see its flowering spread,
Dull-faded, a known decking of her room,
(Wherever that may be then—all words said,
All life made certain then until the tomb!)

Something shall clutch her still of youth and pain,
From that far-thrilled girl-day, and she will see
Its shape grow in that breathless hour again
With all her ordered years were still to be;
From that brown silken flower shall flush in death
Youth with its rosy terrors quivering gay,
And she shall think, set free for one swift breath—
"Ah, yes, I made it on that very day!"

TEA

They've flowers and cakes and candle-light,
  And chair by crowded chair,
And I am very sweet and kind,
  Because I do not care . . .
I think that I am hoping still
  If I am very good
And talk to these around me
  As a courteous lady should

37

The room will softly split across
  And roll to left and right
With all its smiling pasteboard folks
  And colored things and light
And let me run into the grass
And climb a sunset hill,
And find three hours one year ago,
  When I was living still.

DREAM DEATH

What though no folk who saw her knew
  At heart she was Pierrette,
Who went her sober way
In robe and face of gray?
Still down a laughing path of dream
  Her flashing feet were set,
To clink of gold guitars,
Rose-scent and glint of stars!

But when he came who should have known
  Her kin to star and flower
And left her heart unfound,
Nor robe nor mask unbound,
She went her way by daylight still,
  And seemed to live her hour,
Firm hands and lifted head–
Only Pierrette was dead.

TOYS

She loves the flowers, the wind that bends the fir;

When the Spring comes she dances; and her mirth
Comes always when the water laughs to her.
She holds the little daily sweets of earth
On high and pleasures in them; words that sing,
Clear music, lovely faces; all delight
We others pass use-dulled, unnoticing—
The sunrise and the sunset, day and night.

Yet somehow all her woven joys endure
Too perfect, too well-shapen to have rayed
Light-heartedly on her. Oh, I am sure
That once upon a time we do not know
God took away from her—once, long ago—
All life's real, rugged things, too sharp for joys,
And—for she looked at Him still unafraid—
He laid within her hands instead these toys.

Oh, on the gentle day when she goes hence
I hope that for her gay obedience
He has reward for her: that when she dies
He will not send her straight to Paradise.
She knows enough of Paradisal mirth—
Oh, surely He will give her back the earth,
And all its living that He made her miss,
Locked close to life by its most burning kiss,
Clutching decisions, terror-haunted breath,
Great grief, great raptures, passion, birth and death.

MOTHER-PRAYER

"Lord, make my loving a guard for them
    Day and night,
Let never pathway be hard for them;
    Keep all bright!

Let not harsh touch of a thorn for them
    Wound their ease–
All of the pain I have borne for them
    Spare to these!"

So I would pray for them,
Kneeling to God
Night and day for them.

"Lord, let the pain life must bring to them
    Make them strong,
Keep their hearts white though grief cling to them
    All life long,
Let all the joys Thou dost keep from them
    At Thy will
Give to them power to reap from them
    Courage still!"

So I must ask for them,
Leaving to God
His own task for them.

THREE STUDIES FOR A PORTRAIT

I

OLD TALES

Her voice within the darkened room
  Tells on–old jests and tragedies
And little follies of her kin
  And futile old nobilities:

". . . If they had only done," she tells,

"The thing that others said was wise
There would have been no death that year . . ."
  How fast her tiny shuttle flies!

The stiff old pictures on the wall,
  Who were those passionate girls and men
So sure of Youth and Righteousness,
  Look dully on the Now from Then;

And I look past her out the glass
  Where young Today goes to and fro . . .
But all she sees was past a change
  A changeless fifty years ago.

II

THE GRAY MASK

I wish I could not see her heart
  That is so passionate, so young,
For all love-words are said for her,
  All love-songs sung:

Over light griefs her eyes grow wet,
  Over gay silks her eyes grow gay,
She sighs, half-hopeful . . . "I forget
  My hair is gray—"

"I dreamed a lover came for me
  And courted me," she tells, "last night . . ."
Ah, kind dream-lover, who could find
  Such tired eyes bright!

And yet . . . Perhaps some lad in heaven
  Some day shall clasp her soul, and know

Unchanged, the little lass he left
  So long ago.

III

She was so full of restlessness,
  So ceaselessly went to and fro
That it was hard for us to guess
  What thing she wished to find or know:

Only the gifts the gray years brought
  So fretted her on cheek and brow—
Could it have been her youth she sought? . . .
  I hope that she has found it now.

TO A YOUNG GIRL AT A WINDOW

The Poor Old Soul plods down the street,
  Contented, and forgetting
How Youth was wild, and Spring was wild
  And how her life is setting;

And you lean out to watch her there,
  And pity, nor remember,
That Youth is hard, and Life is hard,
  And quiet is December.

A LOST COMRADE

You live as the world would have you do–
Only the sleeping soul of you
Lies unwakened by wind or dew.

Your soul, that thrilled like a harpstring shaken
Dusty hands of the world have taken
And thrust it deeper than life can waken:

You, who quickened our heavy eyes,
Our hearts weighed down beyond will to rise,
With silver shadows of Paradise!

Were it only your heart that the years had broken,
Still should be for a shining token
How your soul had glowed and your lips had spoken–

Were it only your life that was crushed and through! . . .
They have taken the starry soul of you
And hidden it deep from the wind and dew!

DEPARTURE

It was not when I plead with her,
  And on a tragic day
Clung sobbing to her skirts of rose,
  That Youth went away;

O not when from the cruel glass
  My face showed, lined and chill–
Her eyes burnt wild beneath the mask,
  Her pulse hurt me still.

But when I saw young lovers pass,
  And watched them, well-content,

43

Nor felt my eyes grow hot with tears
  To gaze where they went . . .

O then I knew my time was through,
  And pleasured in the day,
At peace to know of Love and Spring
  And Youth gone away.

DISCOVERY

Within my mirror I could see
Last night as I gazed steadfastly
An old strange thing look out at me;

The smile my grandame used to wear;
Line on proud line it faced me there . . .
I had not known it meant Despair.

WOMAN-LORE

Now this is what you learn at last
  Of men beneath the sun,
With all the gates of living passed
  And all the kisses done—
That none are ever old indeed
  And none are very wise,
And they will break you for their need
  Or give you earth and skies:

And out of all between you two
  For all the close years' gain,
The dearest gifts they give to you

Shall come with sorest pain—
(A pain your lips find still untold,
  A joy they cannot see)
Your child they give your arms to hold,
  Your child they grow to be.

THE UNFOUND CITY

(For Alice Brown)

There is a city burning in a dream
  All women know and search for secretly;
The swift rose-hearted flame's eternal stream
  Laps round the changeless towers eternally.

It stands far off above a circling mist. . . .
  Have ye not seen our eyes that seek its light,
Felt the quick sigh between our lips late-kissed,
  Felt our loosed arms yearn toward it in the night?

Gold Helen found it not, nor white Deirdré:
  There is no woman, howso loved, can tell
Of those white changeless dream-towers seen by day,
  Of that flame calyxed, perfect citadel:

We shall not ever know its perfect joy,
  Yet we shall seek it till our years are gone . . .
Eternal Love whose fires shall not destroy
  Eternal Beauty that it beats upon.

THE DARK CAVALIER

I am the Dark Cavalier; I am the Last Lover:
  My arms shall welcome you when other arms are tired;
I stand to wait for you, patient in the darkness,
  Offering forgetfulness of all that you desired.

I ask no merriment, no pretense of gladness,
  I can love heavy lids and lips without their rose;
Though you are sorrowful you will not weary me;
  I will not go from you when all the tired world goes.

I am the Dark Cavalier; I am the Last Lover;
  I promise faithfulness no other lips may keep;
Safe in my bridal place, comforted by darkness,
  You shall lie happily, smiling in your sleep.

PEOPLE

TRAVEL PRAYER

All along the way
  As through the night we go,
I see the little houses
  In lighted row on row—

The flying train goes by
  And sounds its whistle clear,
And all the waiting houses
  They lift their lights and hear:

A thousand homes for miles on miles,
  I press the pane to see;
And each has lights that wait its own
  As my lights wait for me—

All the little homes
  And every one alight!
Lord, keep the people happy
  That wait in them tonight!

HIS MOTHER

He will be cold tonight–
  Always he felt it so.
(Strange not to lift the light,
  Strange not to go,
Softly–for he forgets,
  Careless as glad!–
Drawing the coverlets
  Over the lad.)

Blankly the covers lie,
  Smooth and untossed,
By me the fire burns high,
  Outside is frost . . .
Has it had rest tonight,
  Dear tumbled head?
Lord, I would know–would know
  If he were dead!

It must be cold and wet
  Where our troops lie . . .
(Lord Jesus, spare him yet!
  Let him not die!)
Still here . . . so still . . . and white
  One far clear star . . .
He will be cold tonight,
  Where the troops are.

IN AN OFFICE BUILDING

I went down the old passage
Between the lighted doors
To your lighted door,
Knowing that I should find you there,
Find your swift smile and quickened words,
Comfort and welcome there,
Guardianship and greeting,
As is has always been
As it shall always be.

And suddenly
As my hand touched the door, I knew,
Knowing you quick and warm
And waiting me
That I should dream, some far-off night from this
Of coming down this passageway to you
Between the lighted doors
To your lighted door
Knowing that I should find you there,
And opening, find
An empty frightening place
And you away,
And wake
Remembering you were dead.

GOD'S PLACES

I said, "I am so tired of all the old tired faces
    In the crowded places,
I tire of all the weary steps that cross and beat

Down the long swift street:"
I said, "I will return into my own still room,
    Thick with peace and gloom."

I said, "I will summon up the still bright streams
    Of my trooping dreams,
Whose faces are as weariless and calm and young
    As a bird-note sung,
Who drift along with sunset-colored robes outblowing,
    Of all need unknowing."

And then . . . the sun shone cloudless, and the wind blew fleet
    Down the long swift street
And through the windowed canyon's end the sky's sweet blue
    Shone unwearied through,
And I said, "But I must stay, for see, my brother's faces
    Here in God's own places!"

PEOPLE

(For Jessie Rittenhouse)

I am so sorry for them all
Whose ceaseless footsteps rise and fall
Along earth's highways endlessly,
The people in the world with me;
Who have had dreams, and yet must take
The gifts life has for men awake;
Who build their lives each day anew
On hopes they know cannot come true,
Who walk the world till sleep, and then
At dawn must walk the world again;
Who ask God's favors, knowing still
He does not break His changeless will

For any faulty changing cry
Of men He makes to live or die. . . .

I am so sorry for them all,
So sorry! Until I recall
How life's adventure swings afar
Beyond tomorrow like a star,
And how our dreams paint golden-bright
Gray working-day and sleeping-night,
And all the love each man who lives
May buy with merely love he gives,

And how it comforts us to pray
Whether God hears or turns away,
And how to work and sleep and wake
Is good for the mere doing's sake:
Till, whether life seem gay or sad,
I am so glad for men—so glad!

A BOY OF THE GHETTO

He goes out with his Dreams
  Through the dingy city square,
Purple-and silver-winged
  They go with him everywhere.

The quarreling hags at the windows
  Have voices unkind, unsweet,
But his Dreams have silver voices
  And starrily-slippered feet;

The workmen push on the pavement
  And laugh and curse as they go,
But he is far with his Dreams

On a road they do not know;

He walks far off with the Dreams
  That whisper and sing beside
And his face is glad and still
  And his eyes are burning-wide;

He goes out with his Dreams
  Through a golden wonder-place
With the light of God in his eyes
  And the peace of God in his face.

LIFE TELLS THE DREAMER

These others ask me little, clamoring
For such imperfect gifts as I can bring;
A crown . . . with thorns along it . . . or much gold
To weigh the heart down with its dragging hold . . .
Or men's loud voices calling on their name,
A little day, then hurt and scorn—called Fame—
Or for one fleeting hour a world made new
Called Love . . . But, Child, these gifts are not for you.

Too clear of sight, you ask things past my hold;
A light beyond the sunlight . . . Fairy-gold . . .
Love ageless and unflawed . . . Faith crystal-true . . .
So, Child, I keep my broken gifts from you,
Leaving instead my only perfect thing,
The Dream these others lose, all-sorrowing,
Still raptured, still all-golden; yours to keep
Till Death my sister's gift, more perfect Sleep.

PRESCIENCE

I went to sleep smiling,
  I wakened despairing–
Where was my soul,
  On what terror-path faring?
What grief shall befall me,
  By midnight or noon,
What thing has my soul learned
  That I shall know soon?

I TELL MY HEART

I tell my heart, to hush her aching
When we are sleeping, when we're waking,
Of things we loved well, she and I,
Upon a time that is gone by:

Heart, now the Spring comes there shall be
A bright and blossoming apple-tree
Against the window-light to swing
Its thousand-petaled flowering;
There is clear water, flickering green,
With shining leaf-brown rocks between
And silver fish that hide and dart
Where we may play too, dear my heart;
And there is sunlight's gold that lies
Warmly on cheek and breast and eyes
And little winds at even-star
That slip from where the pine-trees are . . .
And heart, remember how we heard
At twilight once a wakened bird

Whose notes flung out a silver net
Against flame-rose, flame-violet!

Oh, heart, my heart, still can you lie
Dumb while the wonder-spring goes by?

My heart is very young—some while
Perhaps she may look up and smile.

FULFILMENT

Crossing through Heaven's doors,
  If Heaven may be for me,
I shall not seek gold floors
  Nor jasper wall nor sea;

Out from the streets of gold
  Will branch a wooded way
Like one I knew of old
  When all the world was May:

There shall be dusk to fall
  And winds expectant, sweet,
And sleepy birds to call
  And vines about my feet,

Stars in the night's soft black,
  Leaves that swish soft like rain
And one old hour come back
  And one choice given again.

ONCE I MET HAPPINESS

Once when all the Spring was wild,
  All the leaves dew-pearled,
Once I met Happiness,
  Singing down the world.

She had laughter on her lips,
  Flowers in her hair—
Once I met Happiness—
  Oh, she was fair!

There was yellow sun, I know,
  Scent o' pine that day,
Once she kissed me on the lips,
  Laughed and went her way.

What if all the lights are dim,
  All the flowers furled?
Once I met Happiness,
  Singing down the world!

LOVE SONGS

DENIAL

It never would have hurt God
  To have made the world today
  So that your footsteps turned my way,
So that our two paths crossed—
  But I went wearily up and down
  The streets of the empty-painted town
And a whole day was lost!

Never your footsteps where mine trod,

Never my words to you—
And it all would have been so simple for God,
  So slight a thing to do!

THE MASTERS

You have taught me laughter,
  Joyousness and light,
How the day is rosy-wild,
  Star-enthrilled the night:

Maybe God can teach me
  After you are gone
How to bear the blackened night
  And the dreadful dawn.

I SAID, "LOVE IS GONE"

I said, "Love is gone;
  I need bear no more
Terrible dawn
  And midnight sore
Hungering dreams
  I cannot keep
And fever-streams
  Across my sleep . . ."

And the sun went down,
  And the day burned black
Over the town
  And Love came back
And my heart was burned

With fire and pain—
But Love had returned,
Had returned again!

VAIN HIDING

I said: "I shall find peace now, for my love has never been
  Here in the little room, in the quiet place;
The walls shall not quiver around me, nor fires begin,
  And I shall forget his voice and perhaps his face
  And be still for a little space."

But the thought of my love beat wild against the silencing doors
  There in the quivering air, in the throbbing room,
Till his step strode quick and light against the echoing floors
  And the light of his voice was there for the placid gloom
  And his presence a shed perfume.

So I said: "There is no peace more, for the place can never be
  Where the thought of him cannot come, cannot burn me thro',
For the thought of his touch is my flesh, and his voice is a voice in me,
  And what is the use of all you may say or do
  When love is a part of you?"

"MARY, HELPER OF HEARTBREAK"

Well, if the thing is over, better it is for me,
The lad was ever a rover, loving and laughing free,
Far too clever a lover not to be having still
A lass in the town and a lass by the road and a lass by the farther
hill—

Love on the field and love on the path and love in the woody glen—
(Lad, will I never see you, never your face again?)

Ay, if the thing is ending now I'll be getting rest,
Saying my prayers and bending down to be stilled and blest,
Never the days are sending hope till my heart is sore
For a laugh on the path and a voice by the gate and a step on the shieling floor—
Grief on my ways and grief on my work and grief till the evening's dim—
(Lord, will I never hear it, never a sound of him?)

Sure if it's done forever, better for me that's wise,
Never the hurt, and never tears in my aching eyes,
No more the trouble ever to hide from my asking folk
Beat of my heart at click o' the latch, and throb if his name is spoke;

Never the need to hide the sighs and the flushing thoughts and the fret,
And after awhile my heart will hush and my hungering hands forget
. . .
Peace on my ways, and peace in my step, and maybe my heart grown light—
(Mary, helper of heartbreak, send him to me tonight!)

INTERIM

I have a little peace today,
  And I can pause and see
How life is filled with golden things
  And gracious things for me;

I can go watch the water run
  And smile to feel the air

And love the deep touch of the sun
  And know the world is fair . . .

Oh, hush, my soul, take comfort now
  And sleepy-singing lie
Till Love return to hide the sun
  And veil the earth and sky!

OTHER PEOPLE

I look at all the people
  Who meet me and are gay,
And wonder have they broken hearts
  That hurt night and day?

So I am very kind to them
  Whoever they may be,
Because they may have broken hearts–
  Broken hearts, like me.

AND IF YOU CAME–

And if you came?–Oh, I would smile
  And sit quite still to hide
My throat that something clutched the while,
  My heart that struck my side.

And you would hear my slow words fall,
  (Men do not know!) and say
"She does not love me now at all,"
  And rise and go away.

And I would watch, as quietly
  Your footsteps crossed the sill,
The whole world dying out from me . . .
  And speak on, smiling, still.

I WAS STILL A CHILD

I was still a child
  Till I came to you,
Child-eyes, child-heart,
  Child-lips all too true;

I went silently,
  With all-wondering eyes . . .
"She is old," they said,
  "She is grave and wise."

Came your touch that burned
  Eyes and lips and heart;
There were no more dreams
  I could spin, apart:

Now my lips are gay
  And my heart untold;
"She is young," they say . . .
  I am old–am old!

PEACE

All my days are clear again and gentle with forgetting,
  Mornings cool with graciousness of time passed stilly by.
Evening sweet with call of birds and lilac-rose sun-setting,

And starshine does not hurt my heart nor night-winds make me cry.

I can tie a ribbon now, nor hope of your eyes' pleasure
  Makes its hue intolerable if you come not to see,
I can hear old music now, nor stabbing through its measure
  Come the thoughts I would not have, or tears that need not be.

All my days are placid now, as quiet children slowly
  Pacing down a leaf-locked way that has not dale or hill;
Peace again and mirth again, and dawn and even holy. . . .
  I wish I had your hands in mine, and heartbreak still!

ONE WORSE THING

Last Spring I walked these ways, and a sharp grief walked with me,
For you had broken my heart with a light kiss, carelessly,
And I was young and was new to grief, and could think of no worse thing
Than to walk abroad with a hurting heart and be hopeless in the Spring.

But I am older now, and have lived with grief awhile,
And there's one worse thing than a hurting heart that you have to hide and smile,
For I who know what a hurt heart is, and the thing that grief can be,
I—I have broken a heart with a light kiss, carelessly!

GIVERS

My lover kissed my lips, and his arms went round my body,
But you were kissing the lips of my soul in our own wild garden

Where the rose-colored moon shone down
Through a sevenfold garland of rainbow stars
And a river of clear golden music rippled and thrilled
    In our own place.

My lover gave me worship and faith and swift submission,
You gave me a light word, and a touch, before you went from me,
And an endless demesne where my dreams can live my whole life
through
And a living heart to sing with;
There is never cause for grief or cause for laughter
That I do not run to our country of dreams to tell you,
Wrapped in your living arms among the heavenly roses,
Sure of your smile . . .
You, whose heart is a cluster of seven cold stars!

OLD WINE

If I could lift
    My heart but high enough
    My heart could fill with love:

But ah, my heart
    Too still and heavy stays
    Too brimming with old days.

I TOOK HIS DREAMS

I took his dreams from him,
  Boy-dreams of gold and red,
I gave him sorrows dim,
  White grief, instead, . . .

And for a little space
Joy in my careless face.

I took his hope away,
  Light hope, a foolish thing,
I gave him silence gray,
  Death's comforting . . .
Was it my soul that sighed,
Dead on the day he died?

CERTAINTIES

Whether you live by hut or throne
  Whether your feet tread stone or grass
Comes the one lad you shall never own
  Or the one lass;

Whether you've pence to spend or gold,
  Whether you've toil or time to weep,
Comes the one pain that may never be told
  And may never sleep;

Whether you weep or mock in pride,
  Whether you tell or still deny,
Comes the one scar that your heart shall hide
  Till the day you die!

WISE PEOPLE

I think that we are very strong and wise,
  Mocking at love and at the grief thereafter, . . .
For sometimes I forget him in your eyes

And sometimes you forget her in my laughter.

UNFAITH

You hid the love in your eyes—
  How could you think I knew?
It was only a step to his comforting
  From the hurt of you.

For even a woman's eyes
  Grow tired of tears—
It was so long a way to look
  Down the naked years!

And I had rest from heartbreak
  And I had peace from pain. . . .
Why do you have the love in your eyes
  Again, again?

SONG: KIND ADIEU

Good-by, my dear, good-by—
  You woke my heart to break it,
  So if another take it
Why need you turn or sigh?

New roads are soon to find
  And Heaven may well be sending
  At every highway's ending
A lass that will be kind:

Good luck, my lad—good day!

Go singing down the year—
  But as for me, my dear,
I go another way!

LOST COUNSEL

If you were but near me,
  O kindest and best,
I could tell you my trouble,
  And I could have rest;

You would smile and be silent,
  And then you would say
Some word that would still me
  And brighten the day—

Wisest and kindest,
  If you were but near
I could speak of my lover,
  My doubt and my fear,

You would show me my pathway—
  But what shall I do,
Wisest and kindest?
  My lover is you!

I DID NOT KNOW

I did not know that I should miss you,
  So silver-soft your loving came,
There were no trumpets down the dawning,
  There were no leaping tides of flame . . .

Only a peace like still rain falling
  On a tired land with drought foredone,
Only a warmth like light soft-lying
  On a shut place that has not sun.

I did not know that I should miss you . . .
  I only miss you, day and night,
Stilly, as earth would miss the rainfall,
  Always, as earth would miss the light.

AN AFTERNOON

This was one of the dreary whiles
When a woman sits and smiles
Wishing all the talk was over,
Inward thought a weary rover . . .
But my lips smiled vividly—
Ah, the women could not see
How my hand in yours lay warm
Through wide miles of sun and storm
(Far away, dear, did you know
That I smiled to feel it so?)

And my eyes burned bright, elate,
Into theirs of drearier fate,
Seeing your eyes' lovingness
Into mine smile deep and bless
(Far away, love, did you see
On your eyes mine lovingly?)

While between the words they made,
Weary words, I think, dull-weighed,
We were talking each to each—

Why, too short for all our speech
Was the lingering afternoon,
Throbbing fast and vanished soon

(Far away, love, did you hear
All I whispered in your ear?)
And they said–I heard them say–
"What it is to be young and gay!
How she pleasured in the day!"

THE WOOD-PATH

The little wood-path wandered
  Green and brown and gay
Up a hill and down a hill,
  Through a dew-wet way.

It slipped beneath the pine-trees
  Where the winds blew sweet,
Past goldenrod and feverfew
  And fields of whispering wheat;

So far and wide it wandered,
  So many a dusk-sweet way,
I thought the little wood-path
  Was guiding me astray–

But oh, the little wood-path
  It knew, it was wise,
It led me to your waiting arms,
  To your lips, your eyes!

WARNING

As long as you never marry me, and I never marry you,
There's nothing on earth that we cannot say and nothing we cannot
do—
The flames lift up from our blowing hair, the leaves flash under our
feet
When once in a year or a score of years our hands and our laughters
meet!

For east and west through a sorry world we pass with our joy to sell,
And they that buy of our song and jest they praise us that we do
well,
But few can sell us the mirth they buy, and few be that know a
song,
And for all of the praise of the kindly folk, their speeches are over-
long!

But two of a trade, one always hears, might get in each other's way,
And you might be wanting to sing, God wot, when I desired to play,
(Oh, it's rather a danger with folks like us and our sparks that are
flying free)
But I never, never must marry you, and you never must marry me!

Now when we take breath from songs at last, to be what the rest
call dead,
They'll sigh, "Ah, noble the songs they made, and noble the jests
they said!"
And they will inscribe on our monuments regret that our day is
done—
But we will be off in an excellent place, and having most excellent
fun—

Oh, very proud from a golden cloud you'll stride in your crown and
wings,
Till you hear my little earthly giggle behind my gold harpstrings;

And you'll toss your gilt theorbo down on the nearest star or moon,
And carry me off on a comet's back for long, wild afternoon;

And while we're lashing the comet up till it misses St. Michael's
Way,
And laugh to think how the seraphs blink, and what the good saints
will say,
We'll heave a little sigh of content—or a wistful one, maybe—
To know that I never can marry you, and you never can marry me!

Margaret Widdemer – A Concise Bibliography

Poetry Collections
The Factories, With Other Lyrics (1915)
The Old Road to Paradise (1918)
Cross Currents (1921)
Little Girl and Boy Land (1924)
Ballads and Lyrics (1925)
Collected Poems (1928)
The Road to Downderry (1931)
Hill Garden (1937)
Dark Cavalier (1958)

Children's Fiction
Winona of the Camp Fire (1915)
Winona of Camp Karonya (1917)
You're Only Young Once (1918)
Winona's War Farm (1918)
Winona's Way (1919)
Winona on her Own (1922)
Winona's Dreams Come True (1923)
Binkie and the Bell Dolls (1923)
Marcia's Farmhouse (1939)

On Writing

Do You Want to Write? (1937)
Basic Principles of Fiction Writing (1953)

Memoir

Golden Friends I Had (1964)
Summers at the Colony (1964)
Jessie Rittenhouse: A Centenary Memoir-Anthology (1969)

Adult Fiction

The Rose-Garden Husband (1915) (Filmed in 1917 as 'A Wife on Trial')
Why Not? (1916) (Filmed in 1918 as 'A Dream Lady')
The Wishing Ring Man (1919) (Filmed as 'The Wishing Ring Man')
The Boardwalk (1919)
I've Married Marjorie (1920)
The Boardwalk (1920)
The Year of Delight (1921)
A Minister of Grace (1922)
Graven Image (1923)
Charis Sees It Through (1924)
Gallant Lady (1926)
More Than Wife (1927)
Loyal Lover (1929)
Rhinestones (1929)
All the King's Horses (1930)
The Truth About Lovers (1931)
The Pre-War Lady (1932)
The Years of Love (1933)
Golden Rain (1933)
The Other Lovers (1934)
Eve's Orchard (1935)

Back to Virtue, Betty (1935)
Songs for a Christmas Tree (1935)
This Isn't the End (1936)
The Singing Wood (1936)
Marriage is Possible (1936)
Ladies Go Masked (1939)
Hand on Her Shoulder (1939)
She Knew Three Brothers (1939)
Someday I'll Find You (1940)
Lover's Alibi (1941)
Angela Comes Home (1942)
Constancia Herself (1945)
Let Me Have Wings (1945)
Lani (1949)
Red Cloak Flying (1950)
Lady of the Mohawks (1951)
The Great Pine's Son (1954)
The Golden Wildcat (1957)
Buckskin Baronet (1960)
The Red Castle Women (1968)

www.ingramcontent.com/pod-product-compliance
Lightning Source LLC
Chambersburg PA
CBHW060039050426
42448CB00012B/3076